Simply Living Life

David Jaffin

Simply Living Life

First published in the United Kingdom in 2023 by
Shearsman Books
PO Box 4239
Swindon
SN3 9FN

Shearsman Books Ltd Registered Office
30–31 St. James Place, Mangotsfield, Bristol BS16 9JB
(this address not for correspondence)

www.shearsman.com

ISBN 978-1-84861-856-5

Production, composition, & cover design: Edition Wortschatz,
a service of Neufeld Verlag, Cuxhaven/Germany
E-Mail info@edition-wortschatz.de, www.edition-wortschatz.de

Title photograph:
Hannelore Bäumler, Munich/Germany

Printed in Germany

Contents

9

With continuing thanks for
Marina Moisel
preparing
this manuscript

and to Hanni Bäumler
for her well-placed
photograph

If I had to classify my poetry, it could best be done through the classical known "saying the most by using the least". The aim is thereby set: transparency, clarity, word-purity. Every word must carry its weight in the line and the ultimate aim is a unity of sound, sense, image and idea. Poetry, more than any other art, should seek for a unity of the senses, as the French Symbolists, the first poetic modernists, realized through the interchangeability of the senses: "I could hear the colors of her dress." One doesn't hear colors, but nevertheless there is a sensual truth in such an expression.

Essential is "saying the most by using the least". Compression is of the essence. And here are some of my most personal means of doing so turning verbs into nouns and the reverse, even within a double-context "Why do the leaves her so ungenerously behind". Breaking words into two or even three parts to enable both compression and the continuing flow of meaning. Those words must be placed back together again, thereby revealing their inner structure-atomising.

One of my critics rightly said: "Jaffin's poetry is everywhere from one seemingly unrelated poem to the next." Why? Firstly because of my education and interests trained at New York University as a cultural and intellectual historian. My doctoral dissertation on historiography emphasizes the necessary historical continuity. Today we often judge the past with the mind and mood of the present, totally contrary to their own historical context. I don't deny the past-romanticism and classical but integrate them within a singular modern context of word-usage and sensibility. Musically that would place me within the "classical-romantic tradition" of Haydn, Mozart, Mendelssohn, Brahms and Nielsen but at the very modern end of that tradition.

My life historically is certainly exceptional. My father was a prominent New York Jewish lawyer. The law never interested me, but history always did. A career as a cultural-intellectual historian was mine-for-the-asking, but I rejected historical relativism. That led me to a marriage with a devout German lady – so I took to a calling of Jesus-the-Jew in post-Auschwitz Germany. For ca. two decades I wrote and lectured all over Germany on Jesus the Jew. Thereby my knowledge and understanding of both interlocked religions became an essential part of my being. History, faith and religion two sides of me but also art, classical music and literature were of essential meaning – so many poems on poetry, classical music and painting.

Then Rosemarie and I have been very happily married for 61 years now. Impossible that a German and Jew could be so happily married so shortly after the war? I've written love poems for her, hundreds and hundreds over those 61 years, not only the love poems, as most are, of the first and often unfulfilling passion, but "love and marriage go together like a horse and carriage". Perhaps too prosaic for many poets?

When did I become a poet? My sister Lois wrote reasonably good poetry as an adolescent. I, only interested in sports until my Bar Mitzvah, a tournament tennis and table-tennis player, coached baseball and basketball teams, also soccer.

My sister asked whether I'd ever read Dostoyevsky. I'd only read John R. Tunis sports books and the sports section of the *New York Times* so I answered "in which sports was he active?" She said, rather condescendingly, "If you haven't read Dostoyevsky, you haven't lived." So I went to the library for the very first time and asked for a book by this Dostoyevsky. I received *Poor People*, his first book, that made him world famous. My mother shocked to see me reading and most especially a book about poor people said, "David, don't read that it will make you sad, unhappy – we, living in Scarsdale, weren't after all, poor people. From there it went quickly to my Tolstoy, Hardy and so on. In music it started with the hit parade, then *Lost in the Stars*, then the popular classics and with 15 or 16 my Haydn, Mozart, Schütz, Victoria ... And then at Ann Arbor and NYU to my artists, most especially Giovanni Bellini, Van der Weyden, Georges de la Tour, Corot and Gauguin ...

But it was Wallace Stevens' reading in the early 50s in the YMHA that set me off – he didn't read very well, but his 13 Ways of Looking at a Blackbird, Idea of Order at Key West, Two Letters (in *Poems Posthumous*), Peter Quince at the Clavier, The Snowman ... and the excellent obituary in *Time* magazine plus the letter he answered some of my poems with compliments but "you must be your own hardest critic". That pre-determined my extremely self-critical way with a poem. Please don't believe that prolific means sloppy, for I'm extremely meticulous with each and every poem.

My poems were published in the order written and I'm way ahead of any counting... The poem is a dialogical process as everything in life. The words come to me not from me, and if they strike or possibly join-a-union then I become desparate, read long-winded poets like Paz to set me off – he's very good at odd times. Those poems need my critical mood-mind as much as I need their very specially chosen words – not the "magic words" of the romantics, but the cleansed words of Jaffin – Racine used only 500 words. My words too are a specially limited society, often used, but in newly-felt contexts.

O something very special: I have a terrible poetic memory. If I had a good one as presumably most poets, I'd write say one poem about a butterfly, and every time I see/saw a butterfly it would be that one, that poem. But I forget my poems, so each butterfly, lizard, squirrel... is other-placed, other-mooded, other-worded, other-Jaffined. That's the main reason why I am most certainly the most prolific of all poets.

Shakespeare is the greatest of us: his sonnets live most from the fluency and density of his language. I advise all future poets to keep away from his influence and the poetic greatness of The Bible.

Yours truly
David Jaffin

P. S.: As a preacher the truth (Christ) should become straight-lined, timelessly so, but as a poet it's quite different. What interests me most are those contradictions which live deeply within all of us, not only in theory, but daily in the practice. And then the romantics have led me to those off-sided thoroughly poetic truths that mysteriously not knowing where that darkened path will lead us.

Life is *(4)*

a) more important

than whatever

man create
s because

b) life breathe

s the ever-re

freshing un
fathomable

spirit of The

c) Creator himself

Whatever we
create remain

s at best a

d) weak and unsub

stancial imitat
ion of His al

ways original-
initiative

s.

"Friendship at first sight" *(Erich Kästner) (3)*

a)encompass

ing all–four–

b) of-us despite

age differen

ce it became
less a quest

ion of sight

c) than a common

ground of re
ligious and

personal–se
lectivity.

Just keep *(4)*

a) on writing He

needn't be cer

tain of that
voice itself

b) whether his

own or Poem's

or outside
the realms of

our knowing

c) the why and

where because
it created a

unifying rhy

d) thmic-flow

as the Isar
at Bad Tölz

a shallowing–
brightness.

"One shouldn' (5)

a) t talk with

strangers" a

parental warn
ing that has

b) carried-over

generation–

wise Then we
shouldn't

talk at all

c) because not

only so–to–
say unmet–per

sons remain
strangers

d) but at-the-

heart–of–the

matter if
duly account

e) able we're

often estrang

ed from our
own very–selv

es.

Is the once- *(4)*

> *a) time-death of*
>
> all the dino
>
> saurs of
> life itself

> *b) on land and*
>
> on sea an
>
> habitual warn
> ing against
>
> our helpless

> *c) ly claiming*
>
> what The Good
> Lord created
>
> beginning and
> end of life

> *d) itself with*
>
> that myster
>
> ious love-ap
> pealing heart
>
> ful-center
> piece.

Robots *(3)*

a) When teaching

and learning

becomes noth
ing more than

an impersonal

b) transfer of

necessary
information

then we stud
ents become

nothing more

c) than more ob

jects which
could be sub

stituted for
robots as

well.

Is it really *(3)*

a) true that Montre

al's becoming

an underground
city without

b) natural sun

light but only

artificial
ly bright

If so then
we've not only

c) denied the crea

tion itself

but the poetry
of natural–

expressive
ness.

Answering *(3)*

a) Einstein reali

sing better
than we the

perfection

b) of The Creat

ion itself
while denying

a personal
God Why then

did that High

c) er Being take

such a creat
ive effort

without assur
ing a recept

ive–response.

It took a (4)

a) knowledge

of Hitler's

diabolical
aims to awak

b) en the Jewish

pacifist Ein

stein to lett
er President

Roosevelt
the start of

c) what would be

come the atomic

bomb ironical
ly only funct

ional after
Hitler and his

d) Jewish-free

diabolical

empire had been
totally destroy

ed.

Why have sun (3)

a) sets including

that beer-ap
propriating

one in Florida
become for

b) most of espec

ial importan

ce whereas
the far more

positively
future-orient

c) ed sun-rise

s mostly ans

wered with a
continuing

sleepful-dark
ness.

A 2nd Childhood (4)

a) Old age can

also be con

sidered as a
2nd childhood

b) perhaps because

simple elemen

tal tasks as
walking upright

even long–

c) time remain

needful–learn
able Because

the future
seems so

d) vastly-spac

ious Because

beginning
and end re

main unmistak
ably samed.

Almost inter (3)

a) *changeably-e*

qual If man

and woman
have become al

b) *most inter*

changeably-e

qual why have
n't I despite

a self-perpet
uating love

c) *of little*

children re

mained without
that long-a

waited mater
nal-instinct.

Old age democ (3)

a) racy One could

call it part

of a democrat
ic process

b) as each day

we awake pain

ed usually
somewhere

s else The
exact place

c) seems hardly

relevant be

cause the ef
fect's most al

ways quite si
milar.

"Be satisfi (5)

a) ed with what

you have"

Each warm pre-
spring late

b) February

day another

shut-down
picturesque

laked river
ed or histor

c) ic towns mapp

ed-out for

country din
ing Corona

doesn't allow
We appear never

d) theless satis

fied with what

we have usual
ly no more

than an ice

e) cream cone'

s licked-down
tastiness

es' cooling-ef
fects.

Small talk *(4)*

a) if carefully

guided could

grow in to
something

b) big meaning

ful Don't let

yourself be
allured with

tentative

c) uncertaint

ied beginning
s Flavour it

from the start

d) with your own

still ripen
ing if not al

ways timely-
accord

s.

This time *(3)*

a) our 4th conse

cutive outing

to a small
lake we often

b) summered

through with

the coolness
of our time-

suspending
thoughts now

c) totally fenc

ed-off from

a pre-awaken
ed express

iveness.

Neil at 83 *(4)*

a) my several

times class

mate-friend
as a loco

motive still

b) puffing with

pleasurable
future-plan

s growing e
ver younger

by-the-day

c) while I his

slightly
younger friend

reinsured with
113 mostly o

ver-sized poet

d) ry manuscript

s that will
leave their

mark if only
on the print

ed-page.

Origins *(3)*

a) Where does

it begin

with The Word
or the pen

b) in perpetual

dialogue

until this
late February

c) sun has sit

uated itself
for perman

ent–expecta
tion

s.

Retimed *(3)*

a) When age

has final

ly freed us
from work

b) day responsi

bilitie

s and we
become in

creasing

c) ly retimed

to nature'
s own rhy

thmic-call
ings.

Master of *(7)*

a) patience Death

has become

the true mas
ter-of-pat

b) ience await

ing time's

pre-determin
ing calling

s It knows

c) those false-

starts as
well two-tim

ed for Ingo
the closed

d) door instead

of an opened-
receptivity

Sometimes
it's greet

e) ed with a sigh-

of-relief

though it
has also

learned to

f) become fear

ed as with
Michael W.

when an o

g) therwise long-

life-span has
become pre-mat

urely dead-
ended.

Many-sided (3)

a) Some essent

ial poetic–

themes have
become repetit

b) ively-sourced

not only be

cause of the
poet's lesser

remembrance-
claims but

c) also because

they've be

come so many-
sided perspect

ived.

A hopeless (6)

a) cause It's be

come a hope

less cause as
with Puschkin

b) and Du Fu for

example their

subtle-origin
al greatness

proclaimed "un

c) translate

able" I keep
reading them

over and o
ver again un

d) able to de

cipher sign

s of their
(in translat

ion at least)

e) hidden-great

ness My last
ing hope be

ing with my e
ven more un

f) translate

able poems

that English
will remain a

kind of univer
sal–language.

My long dead *(10)*

a) once close

friends as
Michael Butler

and Hans Eis

b) ler I tend

to remember
in particular

ly important
(while so char

c) acteristic)

situation

s Hans for ex
ample took

the same seat

d) when I lectur

ed in his home
town When dead

that seat re
mained his

e) actively re

sponsive though

always vacant
With Michael

his repeated

f) wish that his

honorary
doctoral speech

es would be
published be

g) fore his death

and also that

he and Jean
could be en

abled to at

h) tend my 70th

birthday party
before his dead

ly cancer would
speak the last

i) (ing) word

He appeared

then in a
totally new

j) guise full of

witty spontan

eous and off-
hand observat

ions.

False starter (3)

a) s These con

tinually less

ening quanti
ty of insect

b) s off to a

false start

with an ob
viously false

ly-timed date

c) book free-fly

ing at least
a month be

fore their ex
pected-appear

ance.

"When his (3)

    a) patience run

    s out" anoth

    er of those
    off–the–mark

    b) expression

    s Frankly pat

    ience should
    hardly be en

    dowed with
    running be

    c) cause it re

    mains (as far

    as I've exper
    ienced) still–

    standing.

The Good (3)

a) Lord must

have just

loved color
ings These

b) tiny winter

ed so fine

ly intricate
ly-colored-bird

s impression

c) ing perhap

s their short-
ranged time

ly-appearing
start-down

s.

Glazunov and *(3)*

a) Miaskovski two

proficient

and in Germany
little known

string

b) quartets writ

ers Miaskovski'
s the stronger

more original
lyrically in

tense and con

c) trapunctual

ly better e
quipped of the

two Why so
seldom perform

ed here.

Why have so (4)

a) many 19th and

20th century

prominent Jew
ish and other

b) *wise writers*

found a–new–

life–in–Christ
perhaps because

Jesus' crucifix
ion offers for

c) *giveness for*

those willing

to accept as
egoistic and

sinful their
former ways

d) *And because His*

resurrection

remains the
only answer to

death's totali
tarian domain.

Saint Corona (5)

a) has remained

Queen of the

World and Queen
of our Time

b) s for about

a year now

Nothing's to
be done with

out consider

c) ing her oft

enigmatic
reaction Will

her deadly
reign ever be

d) come complete

ly dead–end

ed Or will
her children

take-over the

e) power in their

hands when
she's finally

deceased.

Why doesn' (4)

a) t the good

and all–power

ful God inter
vene we so

b) often heard

relative to

Hitler's Satan
ic reign Be

cause for

c) some reason

of His own
He wanted us

to overcome

d) a regime legit

imately and
democratic

ally–elect
ed.

Who could *(3)*

a) have it better

a good faith

ful and beauti
ful wife daily

b) at my side

and with poem

s that seem
to have been

written just

c) to suit my ex

pressive

ness Who
could have it

better.

Was it an (4)

a) intruder All

the others

for days pro
fusely ground-

b) based only in

yellow and

white Was it
an intruder

(as I often

c) feel myself)

Jaffin-like
in blue the

first crocus
but perhaps

not so self-

d) conscious

of its in
stinctive

primary-
claim

s.

Why the Europ (4)

a) ean Union came

almost last for

the various
anti-Corona

vaccination
s despite a

b) continual 27

nation individ

ual search for
a suitable

scape-goat
Whereas Is

rael a main

c) ly Jewish nat

ion – and
arent't Jews

still thought
of as particul

arly money-
minded paid 3

d) times the

normal price

to keep (es
pecially of old

er citizens)
safe and a

live.

Confucius (5)

a) once again

(as up until

1912) the
most relevant

b) and genuine

ly Chinese

thinker –
(Buddhism was

imported from

c) India) doesn'

t quite fit-in

to the up-to-
date spirit-

of-the-times

d) especially

with his dis
like of women –

though married
and with two

e) children hard

ly if ever refer

s to them –
Women's live

s matter too.

Kierkegaard (4)

a) 's despica

ble treatment
of a woman

he loved and

b) loved him

dearly suppos
edly to save

her from a
family of de

c) pressive soul-

lengther

s would cause
one to question

d) the valid

ity of his so

falsely-exampl
ed minister

ial-behavior.

Late Febru *(3)*

a) ary's return

ing once a

gain to its
supposed

b) ly genuine

wintered-re
putation

cold and grey
despite the

otherwise

c) ground-based

misleading
spring pre-

determining-
flowering

s.

Judaism' *(3)*

a) s oft higher-

levelled but

less knowledge
able view-of–

b) women pedestal

s them to

such a dis
tancing height

that only

c) through them

genuine Jewish
ness become

s inherit
ed.

Why has grey (3)

a) *(gray) 2 al*

ternate spell

ings though
individual

ly separate

b) *ly used in*

otherwise
contexts Is

the one Eng
lish the o

ther Ameri

c) *can or has*

the weather
claimed its

habitually
so twin-en

dowed double-
talk.

For Aron *(4)*

a) Sport school

s here very
demanding a

full competan

b) cy in an ex

tremely wide
range of

practical
and theoreti

c) cal pursuit

s that I be

gin to wonder
why soccer

d) still remain

s the nation

al past-time
season-in sea

son-out.

Hardly recogni *(4)*

a) ble You wouldn'

t have liked

or recognized
me then pre-

b) adolescent

unanimous

ly voted The Best
Camp Spirit

more talk than
talent but so

c) excited for

the cause it

self in what
ever sport

that at time
s I even grew

d) tired of lis

tening to my

exaggerate
d mouth-

sense.

"Normalcy" (3)

> *a) Those numer*
>
> ous 19th and
>
> 20th century convert
> s to Christ

> *b) ianity such*
>
> a peculiar
>
> lot as most
> good poets
>
> remain even
> to this day

> *c) that I begin*
>
> to question
>
> my own now
> reconsidered–
>
> "normalcy".

Defense-mech (4)

a) anisms Why have

most psycho

therapists
lower–levell

b) ed what they

call defense–

mechanism
s We all need

them the more
varied the

c) better self-

stabilising

Yes "naked
we came in

to this world"
Defense mechan

d) isms protect

ively clothe

us against
a full–assort

ment of poten
cial–danger

s.

Railway track (4)

a) s If you

fully contem

plate those
innumerable

b) tracks lead

ing-out from

Grand Central
Station you

may begin

c) to realise

just how var
ied our way

s have be
come even for

d) those tracked-

with–us al

most same–
direction

ed.

Turning-o *(4)*

a) ver-the-page

At times it

becomes necess
ary to turn–

b) over-the-page

to what's en

tirely fresh
ly-endowed

Many of us
become too

c) often attend

ant to parti

cular recurr
ing problem

s like those

d) old diamond

needles stuck
in to a repet

itively-reviv
ing-nowhere

s-ahead.

Call it a *(4)*

a) know-how rhy

thmic-pleas

ure these short
but fully

b) slept-through

afternoon
ed silent-

spells reviv
ing one's

c) lessening

strength e

ven rhymed
to a famil

d) iarity with

these short-

length poet
ic-impuls

ings.

1938–41 *(3)*

a) This knott

ed wooden room
may once have

seemed painted
with the sold

b) iered forego

ings of its

short-timed
creator Rose

marie's un
known-father

c) with a dis

tant Moscow–

preception
but briefly–

in-mind.

Longish poem *(3)*

a) s certainly

not of my

making most
always leave

b) me contemplat

ing why such

a route hadn'
t been short–

c) cutted even

before its

pre-determin
ing dialogued–

inception.

Posthumous (7)

a) Yes I would

most certain
ly be surpri

sed if by
some means

b) and matter

I could con

tinue to be
lived through

by our son

c) s and grand

children The
poetry's the

best living–
bet The German

d) prayers 2ⁿᵈ-in-

line and those

77 recorded
biblical lect

e) ures despite

their estrang

ed German still
pushing-for

ward My father

d) played-it-safe

with those

Jaffin chair
s at Columbia

and The Law
School although

g) the sitting

themselves

won't-be-
his-for-the

naming.

The wrong (6)

a) train? He did

n't realise

it at first
but it wasn'

b) t his usual

train He re

cognised no
one while the

few time
s this train

c) stopped in

towns he'd

never heard
of The lang

uage spoken

d) on the train

wasn't his
own "Last

stop" the con
ductor called

out in a loud

e) but very dis

tant foreign-
languaged

voice He got

f) up went out

into a world
that would

become in
time really

his own.

I'm not (4)

a) the only one

deeply attrac

ted to Christ
ian culture

b) especially

its music

literature
and painting

without real
ising it would

c) become in its

own way a

preparation
for his God-

given calling-
post-Ausch

d) witz Germany

preaching

INRI Jesus
Christ King

of the Jew
s.

"Leap Year" (4)

a) Today's Febru

ary 28th last

day of this
so-called

b) winter month

Next year I

believe a
"leap year"

As Mark Twain'

c) s famous frog

leaping over
long stretch

es of America'
s Manifest Des

d) tiny and per

haps of a

one-dayed
time as

well.

Christen (3)

a) ing's not e

nough like

signing–up
for that faith–

list topped–

b) off as a cho

colate sundae
with nuts and

whipped cream
the parishes'

welcoming ap

c) plause It's

become little
more than a

one–time cere
monial dress–

rehear
sal.

Only later *(4)*

a) did he real

ise he'd miss

ed the last
boat to what

and where
became only

b) afterward

s an existen

cial question
It became as

my one-time
in Eastern

then Communist

c) Germany They'

d taken me a
side at the

only American
in our church

group Took my

d) wallet and

passport in

terviewed
me in a small

and desparate
ly quiet

room.

Uninhabited (5)

a) houses New neigh

bors across the

poet's window
ed–word–way

b) The previous

ones we'd

both become
suspicious

of simply
packed–up and

c) left leaving

for weeks-on-

end that dark
ened house

Uninhabited
houses awaken

d) for some a

ghost-like

fear of the
unknown

why and where

e) that grows in

time at weed'
s-length in a

carefully plann
ed-garden.

In these (3)

a) Corona time

s the lonely

ones whether
unvisited

b) as my now

dead sister

Doris in an
old-age home

or simply with
out a mate

c) begin even-

more-so to

feel that man
or woman were

not meant to
live alone.

Fully-armed *(4)*

> *a) Now fully*
>
> sourced (arm
> ed) with Dehio'
>
> s mammoth

> *b) cultural guide*
>
> to historic
> monuments
>
> This enormous
> one only for
>
> Munich and

> *c) Upper Bavaria*
>
> that Corona'
> s "Saturday'
>
> s" still not
> opened for
>
> country din

> *d) ing will be*
>
> come at least
> culturally
>
> inordin
> ately–embell
>
> ished.

The late Febru (5)

a) ary sun's been

singing of

the flower
ing pleasure

s of spring

b) while the

cold winter
wind's still

retaining
its former

resolve Few

c) educated Ger

mans feel
fully equip

ped with a
knowledge

d) of American

history and

Chinese cult
ure while the

long out–us
ed Greek and

e) Roman classic

s still re

main an essen
tial part of

their future–
orientation.

Educated? *(6)*

a) Linguistic

facility re

mains a key
element in

b) German educat

ion whereas

we American
s have conquer

ed the world
with our own

c) post-Shakes

pearean lang

uage Education
continues to

be big-letter
ed by us with

d) packed book-

shelves of no

vels historie
s and the like

mostly read
Though on both

e) sides of the

ocean adher

ence to qual
ity books has

become more-

d) than-not limit

ed to those
universi

ty-day
s.

St. Emmeram (5)

a) Here in the

small and in

significant
town of Klein

b) Helfendorf

their priest in

the 7th century
falsely accused

had his eyes

c) bored through

his tongue ta
ken-out and

the rest of his
body mutilat

ed All that of

d) his martyrdom

visually and
even dramati

cally alive to
this very-day

e) The church

remains gift
ed with a

long remem
brance-span.

Miaskovski *(4)*

a) 9th quartet'

s not music

to rest and
possibly sleep–

b) by after a

good noon meal

It's powerful
ly resonating

music that wa

c) kens polyphon

ic current
s within one'

s activating
presence It de

d) mands hearing

the full range

of its voiced–
intransigen

ces.

That full *(2)*

a) moon remained

irresistib

ly there
watching me

through
with its pen

b) etrating

magnetic

calling the
seas to their

tidal-awaken
ings.

Poeming (2)

a) each day

s like nam

ing a new-
born-child

It's become
my day in

b) scribed in

a future

book for
lack of a

personal-
remembran

ce.

A Corona *(7)*

a) church mini-

concert with

readings bibli
cal and o

therwise

b) for organ

and flute a

strange com
bination no

composer I'd

c) ever heard of

had taken-up such
a challenge

either trans
criptions of (which

d) are for me legit

imate only if

done by the
composer him

self) or 2nd

e) rate music by

unknown or
little known

composers It
turned out to

f) be both while

the excellent

ly chosen reading
s by our gift

ed and aging

g) dean kept me

concentrat
edly-awake for

multiple-con
cealed-mean

ings.

Take an example from (4)

a) In these long-

extended (over
a year now)

b) Corona time

s Only the

weather dare
s persist

on its wind-

c) purposing

course unvac
cinated des

pite the theor
etically allow

ed types una

d) fraid of the

multiple
mutations

England-wise
Brasil-wise

South Africa-
wise ...

Field cross (6)

a) es remain as

a–most–certain–

way of remem
bering Christ'

b) s heroic deed

s done on our

behalf as the
great tradit

ion of relig

c) ious art per

petuated by
Bellini Van

der Weyden and
so many other

d) first rate

painters Yet

our times
seem indiffer

ent to any

e) thing other

than an agnos
tic self-find

ingness also

f) visually express

ed through
those sancti

fied grave
stone

s.

Some theme *(4)*

a) s and the per

sons they re

present should
remain person

b) ally buried un

touched from

their now
sanctified

past No I be
lieve we should

c) n't only re

member their

now idealis
ed soul-find

ings but should
conceal espec

d) ially as a min

ister our own

privately o
therwise in

sight
s.

New born (5)

a) my Nicodemus

christening

text doesn't
mean annull

b) ing the past

by disowning

one's own par
ents or even

helping them annul

c) their own marr

iage New born
means realis

ing one's own
life past pre

d) sent and future

within a new

personal per
spective

through Jesus'

e) sin-annuling

crucifixion

and his fut
ure-perspect

ived resurrect
ion.

It's an old

children'
s trick play

ing one par
ent against

the other
which can cer

tainly endang
er the marr

iage itself.

One can o (3)

a) *verdue one's*

own special

themes That'
s perhaps an

b) *inherent dan*

ger in some

of Miakovski'
s quartet

s but it's
also person

c) *ally meant*

the danger of

overplaying
certain self-

recurring
theme

s.

Some person *(4)*

a) s I know (and

you do as well)

rarely learn
to stop emphasiz

b) ing with their

own voice or

repeticious
ideas Such per

sons also tend

c) to wear some

what extrava
gent cloth

es speaking

d) especially

aloud that
one could hear

them even from
the next room.

Are most

spiders natur
ally gifted

as Mozart
creating their

webs perfect
ly-precision

ed without
need of thor

ough-revis
ions.

The divided British *(4)*

a) Strange that

the painterly
taste of the

b) British accord

ing to The Nation

al Gallery
should be so

home-bred

c) Turner and Con

stable Hogarth
and let's not

forget that
Van Eyck and Hol

d) bein a distant

2nd Whereas in

music they're
more continent

ally-orient
ed.

The great *(4)*

> *a) poetic Tang*
> period in
> China not
> only poetical

> *b) ly high-level*
> led but anoth
> er concern re
> mained at
> least so relev
> ant the lot

> *c) ions and pot*
> tions for o
> vercoming
> death whose
> poisonous
> effects

> *d) remained e*
> ven more dan
> gerous than
> politically-
> engaged–poet
> ry.

The daily *(4)*

a) weather's not

small talk

but bigger
than one real

b) ises effect

ing most essen

tially one'
s changing

moods as the

c) changeable

clouds self-in
volving light–

darkness quite
apparently

d) harmless yet

more than re
levant for

the indecis
iveness of

daily–concern
s.

If we could (3)

>*a) live our life*
>
>backward
>
>s not in an
>ageful–sense

>*b) but in a con*
>
>secutive
>
>day by day
>approach
>
>ing at the

>*c) end what be*
>
>gan as a be
>
>ginning
>death–birth
>
>ed origin
>ed.

Don't press-

your–point–too
hard It might

break as an
old–fashion

ed fountain–
pen.

Mooned to (4)

a) the memory of

S. L. Now that

we've not
only stepped–

on its surfa
cings and

b) certified

its insuffi

cient dead
ness Why does

the moon con
tinue to

voice all the

c) urgings of

all the earth'
s tidal o

ceans and
seas certain

ly not dead
land but still

d) poetically-

voiced witness

ing the ebb
and flow of

the poem's
rhythmic–imag

ining
s.

Red-lines *(14)*

a) We all draw

our own red–
lines whether

we realise

b) it or not

though by
politician

s often dis
regarded

c) Mine most es

pecially with

in the cultur
al–philosophi

cal realms

d) Wagner because

of his 1850
work relative

to the Jews
in music 3

e) years after

Mendelssohn'

s death whom
he earlier ex

tolled as a

f) central influen

ce of his
work Mendels

sohn whose
music he villi

g) fied as with

all Jewish com

posers simply
because of

their Jewish

h) ness Wagner

became for my
eyes and ear

s The First
Nazi Rimbaud

i) whose personal

life as Wagner

s remained vul
garly self–com

mitted Rimbaud

j) the father of

modern poetry
who turned

against poetry
also debasing

k) his own and

continued to

lead an in
famous life

l) Heidigger

because of
his Nazi-sym

pathising
past even

turned again

m) st his Jewish

teacher whose
chair he then

made-his-own
Heidigger

documented

n) through his

own diary re
mained a Nazi

even after
Auschwitz.

Self-criti *(3)*

a) cism So often

(as I contin

ue to wit
ness) those

b) most critical

of other

s find them
selves unable

to turn that

c) focus to the

more person
ally–diffi

cult self–
criticism.

Replica (3)

a) A little

black bird

visitor on
my woodened

b) balcony survey

ing the varied

house and tree
surrounding

landscaping

c) s with much-

the-same pier

cing-eyed
self-endowed

satisfact
ion.

As my car (4)

a) *ing wife A*

secondary

tiny bird
with all

b) *those espec*

ially select

ive–intricate–
coloring

s just land
ed on the o

c) *ther side of*

my support

ive balcony
pecking away

at all those
hardly visi

d) *ble vitamen*

ed–taste some

how remind
ing of my so

caring wife.

Hot and Cold (5)

a) March just

arrived anoth
er of those

transition
al months am

b) plified with

those warming

effects now
perhaps expect

antly more

c) spring-like

appearan

ces Despite its
daily expand

ing light–span

d) sometimes

birthed with
those cruel

reminder
s of winter'

e) s time-hold

ing grasp

a mirror
to our own

self-attend
ing way

s.

What my fa (4)

a) ther consider

ed as "small

persons mak
ing themselve

s especial

b) ly important"

in that case
a policeman

who caught
him going

c) through a

red-light

Such an atti
tude at-odds-

d) end with his

self-professed

liberal demo
cratic self-re

ceptive other-
wiseness.

6 Views *(4)*

a) of Rosemarie

inhabiting

the poet's
window-sill

b) The more I

ponder their

very-being
either 6 to

tally differ

c) ent aspect

s of her own-
singularity

or her aliven

d) ing (each in

its own way)
6 different

ly selected-
background

s.

Is it more (2)

a) a question of

what we as

painters and
poets focus–

upon or put
the-other-way-

b) round Why is

that object

or person fo
cusing us in

such a self–
assuming way.

Who needs *(4)*

a) the circus a

crobats if

you've squir
rels in your

b) own backyard

Our Ulysee

s and Samuel
put-on their

leaping branch-

c) running half-

flying show
in thanks

for their
daily fat-siz

ed walnuts un

d) fortunately

often stolen
by those in

vading over-
sized raven

s.

The European (6)

a) Union It's hard

ly ever possi

ble to achieve
a 27 unifying–

b) agreement

on major issue

s as the far–
too–late achiev

ed vaccinat
ions a laugh

c) ing-stock for

American Chin

ese English
and Israelis a

like The Fren

d) ch will alway

s remain that
self-glorifying

nation The Ger
mans too rich

for wealth–shar

e) ing … that

the so–called
European Union

more in theory
than in fact

will probably

f) never be offi

cially–mapped
with its sin

gular–name.

Comparing (7)

a) doctor's wait

ing rooms a

less recognis
ed sport of

b) aging-person

s Not so

much the
rooms them

selves as

c) the other

patients in
volved in

contagious
fears or per

d) haps only in

preparation

for the usual
5 injection

s Their wall–

e) pictures most

often display
hideous ex

amples of so-
called modern

f) art or breath-

taking mountain

ous or sea-
scapings dis

g) tancing the

perhaps on

coming pain-
suspecting

decision
s.

Is poetry *(4)*

a) a form of

literature

maybe not as
presented

b) today Obama

our past-pre

sident refer
ed to poetry

and then liter

c) ature not the

first time I'
ve heard that

or was he es
pecially touch

ed by that

d) young black

lady whose poet
ry helped

emotional
ise Biden's

inaugurat
ion.

That same *(3)*

a) mirrored-i

mage as when

I was only
8 keeps look

ing back at

b) me wordless

ly saying
"When you're

dead you'll
cease to be

your entire

c) world always

focused on
your own self-

being will
reach its dead-

end".

Question (3)

a) ing Heine Why

must the beau

ties of this
world created

b) by the same

God who sent

Jesus on his
mission of per

sonal redempt
ion be totally

c) denied The i

dea of progress

yes but not
the creation it

self.

Admiring (4)

a) Werfel who

realised the

divinity in
Christ but (so

b) it seems) re

fused to deny

his Jewish i
dentity in

those perilous

c) times I too re

fuse to deny
my historical

Jewish identity

d) while preach

ing The Jewish
God INRI His

own identity-
sake.

We shouldn' (6)

a) t judge but

neverthe

less what
should one

b) say to the

adulterous

Alma Mahler
who as a

femme fatale

c) specialised

in famous men
Mahler Gropius

Werfel (two of
whom were Jewish)

d) while she re

mained some

how inhabited
with more than

a touch of

e) anti-semetism

(or was it
anti-Judaism)

Who as (it
seems) remained

f) faithful to

Werfel during

those long most
dangerous

of time
s.

Must a con (4)

a) version to

Catholicism

become church-
inclusive

I can't ac
cept the holi

b) ness of a

church plag

ued (though
less so than

the Lutheran
one that I

so-to-say re

c) present) with

a tradition
al anti-Juda

ism and anti
semetism Des

pite all at
my heart's

d) depth committ

ed to Luther'
s biblical–

Jesus not an
also-church and

Mary-center
ed faith.

Why those (3)

a) beer-mug pic

ture-book

Floridian
sunsets when

b) I can admire

as today a

Bavarian
sunrise so

c) lightly ap

parent all

dressed in
blue and

white.

It's the (3)

a) *heart's length*

and depth and

the mind's
verified a

b) *cuteness that*

helps deter

mine the qual
ity of one'

s art not so
much as the

c) *romantic*

s would have

it pover
ty sickness

and need.

Ping-pong (3)

a) at our level

of competan

ce establish
es its own

b) sense of rhy

thmic-concen

tration quite
similar in

c) tent to the

poetic dia

logues' most
persisting-

need
s.

Aloneli *(5)*

a) ness That

house across–

the-way will
remain vacant

b) for 2 months

before its new

owners (who
seem quite plea

sant a tradit

c) ional family

of husband
wife and 2

young child
ren though dog

d) less) move-in

Will that house

(perhaps also
helped through

these words)

e) find a mean

s of answer
ing its not-

so-short-
time-aloneli

ness.

Off-balance (4)

a) Men's cloth

s hardly in

terest me
aesthetical

b) ly quite o

therwise my

playboy Uncle
Joshua Surpris

ed yes caught-
off-balance

c) by 3 special

compliment

s for my new
sneakers

my poems could
be called

d) sneaky as well

especially

those oft
watching-out-for

sneaky-ending
s.

Origined (4)

a) Is it true

that in an

artificial
atmosphere

poet's can con
ceive only arti

b) ficial poem

s If so then

a poet can
only imagine

what his sense
s keep him

persistant

c) ly self-cer

taining Can
my "mind's

eye" really
see beyond

this totally

d) artificial

dentist's
waiting room

in to those
realms of un

inhabited
thought-feel

ings.

Trade-marks (5)

a) If as they

say every

person poss
esses his

b) own trade-

mark Where

should mine
be as the

young athlete

c) the question

ing student
the self-con

vincing min
ister or now

d) as the prob

ing-poet

If our own
trade-mark

implies a
life's center

e) could be noth

ing or no

one else
than my dear

Rosemarie.

Spring (3)

a) with its in

herent un

certaint
ies has be

b) come for

most a time

of anticip
ating but

for what
and why It's

c) a time of un

ease and seem

ingly but dif
fusely exper

ienced–expec
tation

s.

Our garden' *(3)*

a) s become wild-

flowered

first in
yellow then

that "snow

b) piercing"

whiteness
finally a

blue to match
the sky's

primary-color

c) ing but then

last but cer
tainly not

least the im
passioned

blood-red.

On those (3)

a) transition

al days in

early March
when it

b) slowly cloud

s–over One

feels as
if shadow

c) ed in one'

s most e

lusively
extending–

past.

One can't

"make-up for
lost time"

Real friend
ships grow

in depth
through

time and com
mon-experien

ce.

One "falls (2)

a) asleep" as

one "falls

in love" Both
impression

an accident

b) al loss-of-

balance
in to a state

of dream-like
impenetra

ble-darkness.

R. P. *(4)*

a) The "easy

way" especial

ly designed
for self–in

b) terest may

achieve in

time a limit
ed sense of

self–fruit
ion But once

c) it becomes

so opportune

primarily
at the cost

of other
s It won't

d) enable one

to discover

an "easy way"
for getting–

out–of–trou
ble.

Telling "the (3)

a) truth the

whole truth

and nothing
but the

b) truth" curr

ents against

our usual ten
dency of re

porting a

c) situation

more-than-
anything-else

for self-in
terest-sake.

Little Franz *(5)*

a) now in pre-

kindergart

en has lin
ed-up in

b) the garden

all of his

most import
ant possess

ions perhap

c) s as a per

sonal mean
s of display

ing his own
sense-of–

d) ownership

But also per

haps because
both of his

parents work
leaving them

e) little time

and effort

for his own
familied–pur

posing.

Do pains *(3)*

a) as trees poss

ess collect

ive under
ground-communi

cative-abilit

b) ies Mine at

least seem
prepared to

take-on-new
assignment

s even at o

c) therwise re

mote place
s of my

body's self-
reassuring-

composure.

Post Ausch (4)

a) witz moralist

s We've a

moralist
ic party here

b) in Germany

that's most

engaged for
the concern

s of disab

c) led children

and other
wise such per

sons Yet they

d) also supp

ort aborting
these same

pre-born per
sons.

It all start (6)

a) s at home

learning to

listen to
the other

b) side of im

portant issue

s The willing
ness to com

promise and

c) accept one's

own responsi
bility for

mistakes Now
at the pre-

d) war level

students in

America Ger
many and else

wheres only

e) willing to

accept speak
ers and pro

fessors of

f) their own

self-identi
fying color

s What's com
ing next?

Pre-design *(7)*

a) ing the fu

ture All those

most interest
ed in pre-de

b) signing the

future should

realise once-
and-for-all

after Corona

c) that all of

our wishful-
thinking

remains in

d) the hands of

forces out
side our own

purposeful-
control One

e) doesn't need

Heine's 8

years of help
lessness a

gainst bed–

f) ridden pain

s to realise
the need for

a comforting

g) and loving

God in disre
gard of all

such ideas–
of-progress.

I don't (4)

a) seem to know

much about

fences But I
do experien

b) ce neighbor

s who greet

us in a most
friendly way

while other

c) s who don't

seem to real
ise our pre

sence even

d) when passing

close-by a
less–than–in

different–re
sponse.

Callings (2)

a) Spring bud

s spring

bloom and
spring flower

ing our post-
wintered

b) eyes with a

wake-up

sense for cele
brate life'

s persist
ent-calling

s.

Of all sea *(4)*

a) sons spring

fashions it

self as the
lightest

b) most trans

parent even

child–like
yet today

it seems

c) weighted with

cool and cloud
ed concern

s It perhap

d) s too often

conceals that
other side

of self–be
ing.

Roofs (3)

a) These 7-hous

ed-roofs win

dowing my
poetic-land

b) scaping ap

pear to be

slanting
my own in

c) sights to a

ground-based

perhaps irre
trievable

bottomness.

5-Timed (4)

a) "He's had

his day" an
expression

implying more-
or-less that

b) "his time's

up" directed

at someone
who seems to

be "over-the-
hill" but

c) one shouldn't

in a good
Christian

d) sense "pour-

it-on-too-

much" or "hit
a man when

he's (really)
down".

Behind that *(3)*

a) less distant

darkening

window may
be inhabit

b) ing a family

situation

that would
well prefer

looking-out
even through

c) a glass-per

spective than

looking-in
to the quick

sand of its
here-and-now.

General *(3)*

a) ly used ex

pression

s can claim
a right-of–

b) way if they'

re correct

ly routed
and precision

c) ed to an ex

acting sense

of not only
here-and–

now.

Colorings *(5)*

a) Strange to-

say for one

"limited" with
a partial

b) color blind

ness those o

therwise re
presented

coloring

c) s take-on a

special mean
ing of their

own Who creat
ed them in

d) the first

place and why

do most all
coloring

s seem con

e) tent with their

not self-cho
sen though com

pelling-appear
ance.

An early March *(3)*

a) afternoon

Space light

and air per
haps the

best means of

b) describing

this early
March after

noon though
lacking a per

manence still

c) activating

a presence
reaching be

yond its
own-time-

telling
s.

Natural heal (3)

a) *ing from pain*

s and sick

ness one of
The Good Lord'

b) *s most preval*

ent ways of

expressing
His guidance

of a creation
whose life-

c) *signs bear*

s his own

most person
al-signa

ture.

To this *(5)*

a) very day new

discoverie

s here on
earth or in

b) the ocean's

depth in the

most remote
of places

of creature
s hardly i

c) maginable

signifying The

Good Lord'
s unlimited

life-im
pulsings while

d) the perhaps

unlimited

reach of
space and un

told galaxie
s proof of

e) The Good Lord'

s unfathom

ably possible
life-intent

ions.

Whatever (4)

a) of the past

I've forgott

en may not
have forgott

b) en me in

dreams that

haunt an o
verheard

time-span

c) or through

those as
Neil who re

member what
I've long

d) since forgot

ten re-birth

ed while perhap
s claiming a

nother iden
tity now.

Unable to (5)

a) forgive as Jew

s and Christ

ians have been
taught because

b) the wounds of

the past open-

up what's even
more personal

ly exposed

c) than the

present day'
s less-con

suming-satis
faction Does it

d) remain possi

ble to harden–
up as the pro

phet Ezekiel
protective

e) against what'

s even more

than he–could–
possibly–real

ise–why.

Two-sided (3)

a) Tensions of

whatever

kind as fear
s themselve

b) s evoke eith

er a self–

delegated
power over

our own help

c) lessness

or activate
a creative

most person
al defens

ive–response.

What one (5)

   a) "might call a-

   capitalist

   ic instinct"
   for "more

   more more"

   b) may evoke a

   most similar
   poetic-re

   sponse as in
   Wallace Steven

   s' late "2 letter

   c) s the "more

   more more" of
   those most

   intimate
   ly quiet-soli

d) tudes Such spec

ial moments
that may never

return if
significant

ly poetised
may retain a

e) newly housed

poetic-rele

vance paged
for touched-

through repet
itive-gain.

These wind (3)

a) s may real

ise their

own special-
callings

b) yet for us

they remain

singular
ly-elusive

coming to

c) going with no

permanent
ly ascribed

homestead
in-sight.

Dentistry (4)

a) requires that

same kind of

concentrat
ion that the

b) poem reserve

s for its

own special
word–obedien

ce That's

c) perhaps why

my dentist'
s become so

short temper

d) ing his come

and go assis
tants in to

but a few
month's stay.

Is it only (3)

a) the eye or

the Shakespear

ean "mind's
eye" that a

wakens a dia

b) logical poet

ic–response

Or can for
example that

momentar

c) ily vacant house

right–across–
the–way inde

pendently

d) begin quest

ioning my poet
ically pre–de

termining
need

s.

Personally sourced (6)

a) If The Good

Lord created
each of us

(even the
so-called

b) identical

twins) in

a most person
al-identifying-

way does that
indicate as

c) well the spec

ial nature

of our own
personally-

sourced faith.

d) Winter return

ed last night
a most cer

tainly unwant
ed-guest But

e) as our own

wants are so

personally-
sourced per

haps we should

f) tacitly accept

winter's irre
trievably

inrevers
ible decis

ions.

Complete (4)

a) ly unherald

ed it's be

ginning to
snow again

b) hardly off-

timed in

early March
yet the pro

fuse flower

c) ings and pre-

timed insect
s must seek

protection
as we do with

d) our Italian

ate rain–pro

tective um
brellas in

mid–July.

My Dina *(3)*

a) Those as my

mother's mo

ther illiter
ate thorough

b) ly practical-

minded ground–

based are
seldom those

receptive
of transcend

c) ental dream

s and a faith

that has stood–
up to rever

sals of most–
any–kind.

Tobey' (3)

a) s Chassidic-

dancers liv

ing-things-up
on our bedroom

b) wall so joy

fully respond

ing that
they seem al

most releas

c) ed from the

canvases' us
ual orderly-

expectat
ions.

This snow (2)

a) origined bey

ond our own

space-limit
ing exposure

s a world
that become

b) s most visual

ly alive at

the touch of
its cold but

melting-trans

parancie
s.

He made the *(3)*

> *a) impression*
>
> of a fisher
>
> man plying
> the deep with

> *b) a hook and*
>
> sinker reach
>
> ing-himself-
> out to that

> *c) unknown but*
>
> neverthe
>
> less self-re
> vealing dark
>
> ness.

What's (5)

a) more self-de

meaning being

daily watched
as Weinberg

b) by Stalin's

secret police

Or express
ing one's deep

est convict
ions to a psy

c) chothera

pist who's pre

determined
in his own

frame–of–re

d) ference

That "I
told you so"

kind of per
son should

e) be avoided

at all possi

ble length
s from ser

ious artist
ic–introspec

tion.

.

She under (3)

a) stood more

intuitive

ly than she
could express

b) word-wise

Few are born

or become
genuine poet

c) s perhaps al

most as few

so intuitive
ly-recept

ive.

It snowed

the night
through

his dream-
enlighten

ing lost-re
membranc

es.

Nothing better (2)

a) than cleaning-

out the over–

stocked and
only partial

ly visible
bookshelve

b) s to redis

cover what'

s become
more than half–

lost from mem
orie's-sake.

Sickness- *(2)*

a) time a shad

owy world of

those diffuse
moments when

one seems

b) only faintly

aware of a
world that's

become distant
ly-obscur

ed.

As I contin (3)

a) ue to forget

more and quick

er than I
learn my life

b) can be conceiv

ed in this

sense as a pro
cess of daily e

rosion Only my
prolific poetic

c) impulsings have

attempted to

create a last
ing balance

between win
and loss.

Two-sided *(3)*

a) This moon'

s now slic

ed right–
down-the-midd

le as two–

b) sided as we

most often
appear as my

simultain
eously hous

ing both the

c) poet and the

person not
always a un

ity of pur
pose and re

sponse.

Prime-time *(6)*

a) Most all-of-

us inhabit

both strong
er and weaker

times My

b) strength be

comes most
efficient

in the morn
ing Rosemarie

c) 's the-later-

the-better

Prime-time
has become

poetry-time

d) if not thor

oughly used
turns-to-waste

Time itself
continues to

e) use each of

us for its

own end We
must use our

f) allotted time

to counter

its unalter
able rhythmic–

flow.

As Mrs Hoff (4)

a) man at 93

surrounded

by 21 grand
sons and grand

b) daughters all

shar a comm
on–faith Such

an unusual
blessing in

c) these agnost

ic self–cen

tered dis
abled times so

much in need

d) of more than

a self–find
ing search

for a perpet
ually–elus

ive–cause.

Sometime (4)

a) s I feel

the harder

the more
strenuous

b) the making

s of these

poems the
less genuine

they reveal

c) themselve

s perhaps
because that

outside voice has
become lesser

d) heard that

the poems re

main but an
intraperson

al–dialogue.

Replacement Therapy *(8)*

a) The so-called

experts claim
that because

of the Corona
pandemie the

b) usual flu-per

iod remained

practically
voiceless

Yesterday

c) my physiother

apist asked
me whether

through his
massages my

hip pains have

d) lessened in

tensity Yes be
cause my oper

ated big toe
has provided

e) greater pain

s I'd almost

forgotten
about my hip

f) ones A slight

remembran
ce of snow

has left this
ground-base

g) garden or

ours somewhat

brightened
for a Satur

day display
of clothed

h) sufficien

ces but at

the cost of
once flower

ing-surface
s.

Church-bell *(3)*

a) calls For many

here it re

mains only
the clear–

b) cool-repetit

ive resonat

ing Sunday church-
bell-calls

c) of a once-

faith now

but just–so–
faintly–re

minding.

It was per (3)

a) haps Wallace

Stevens' "Jan

uary sun" that
enabled me

b) to realise

the poetic-im

portance of
names whether

of times pla

c) ces or per

sons actuali
sing their

ever-presen
ce.

Criticism *(4)*

a) of whatever

kind place

or person
should never

b) lead to a

full knock-

out-blow be
cause we too

realise the

c) importance

of finding-
a-way-out

even of those
two-timed

car stuck-

d) in that win

tered snow
and mud-poss

essive
ness.

Origins *(4)*

a) *Especial*

ly Klee's art
for children

ed–me–back
to a fantas

b) *ied world*

that has still

remained trans
parently-

present Klee'

c) *s finely sens*

ed art sur
faces–us back

to the child–

d) *like-origin*

s of our i
maginative

self–discov
erie

s.

Although (3)

a) now at 83 I'

m apparent

ly safely an
chored new

b) friends and

places revive

in me and in
Poem as well

c) the desire

to dialogue
our newly ex

perienced-
impression

s.

New-and-other *(3)*

a) wise-perspect

ives help re

vive a work

b) of art's oft

hermetical
ly-withholding-

secrets That'
s perhaps the

c) most genuine

raison d'ê

tre for attenta
tive-interpre

tive–artist
s.

Why did con (7)

a) temporarie

s of Vermeer

for example
so under-estim

b) ate his cool

restrained

aesthetic-
qualities

while today

c) the same paint

ings affect
most in-a-to

tally-differ
ent-way Did

d) the changing

times change

the taste as
well but why

new appraisal

e) s may once a

gain reconsid
er his so

specially–

f) sourced-art

Vermeer
remains but one

of dozens of
other-example

g) s Mendelssohn

has experienc

ed several radi
cal change-

of-taste-
s.

For G. H. *(3)*

a) Somewhat

longer narra

tive or
thought poem

b) s require a

natural express

ive-fluency
that flow

s freely to
its own end

c) s not the

tight-grasp

of concentra
ted earlier

Jaffin-poem
s.

Why does (2)

a) the Tang poet

Po chü-i trans

late the best
surely true

If not even
the Chinese

b) know How should

I judge be

ing a non–
translate

able poet my
self.

Why are (3)

a) those poet's high

est–Confucian–

aim to serve
the monarch

well who rare

b) accepts their

advice banish
es them to re

mote areas
when out–of–

favour He may

c) be holy for

them but why
doesn't he

lose his God–
like ephemer

al–shine.

Winter's un (2)

a) expected re

run early in

March some
how remind

ing of an old
but distant

b) friend reappear

ing long af

ter we'd writ
ten-him-off

if only season
ably.

The older (5)

a) we become so

often the more

demanding
mirroring

b) our choice

of friends

concerts food
s and even

post–Corona

c) vacation

ing Does
that reflect

the need for
special priori

d) ties in our

limiting

time–sense
or perhaps

e) a greater

satisfaction

with our pre
sent state-of–

being.

That declin

ing moon's in
sisting light

seems as if
focused on

my own lesser-
time-left

before I also
become appar
ently lost–

from-sight.

A letter- (5)

a) *friend some*

thing entire

ly new for
me with an

b) *American*

Christian

and well–
worded poet

and for year

c) *s an avid*

admirer of
my own verse

The credent
ials seem

d) quite-appro

priate but

can one es
tablish a

e) real friend

ship with an

otherwise
unknown-per

son.

"What makes (2)

a) this day differ

ent from every

other day" a
Passover quest

ion that's
passing o

b) ver me now

an over-siz

ed raven sha
dowing what

ever it's
left-behind.

Two ways *(5)*

a) An every

day pract

ising Christ
ian routin

b) ed to a faith

that may even

offer a full
daily-cover

age Some would

c) feel that as

insuffi
cient requir

ing miracle
s or at least

d) a specially

near-close

ness to The
Living God

Others would
answer "a

e) daily life

with the Liv

ing God what
more do you

really need".

Contrasts (6)

a) For most

it takes a

time to be
come at ease

b) with a new

personal

surround
ing Van Gogh

didn't require

c) more than a

lengthen
ed moment

writing-off
a landscape

d) that contin

ued to poss

ess his inner–
most turmoil

Whereas Gau

e) guin needed

extra–time

to allow that
otherwise

Southern

f) France land

scape to in
vade his en

tire existen
cial–person.

Fluffy *(3)*

a) child-like

clouds per

haps happily
being sent–

b) back-to-

school after

that long
Corona inter

lude Nothing
certains a

c) teacher so

pleasant

ly as child
dren longing

to get-back-
to-school.

Upon 2nd (5)

a) thought a

letter-rela

tionship may
hold more se

b) curely than

a usual one

because a
divergent

personal

c) chemistry

can hardly
become fully

papered-down
but that extra

d) safeguard

can also remain

as a wall
dividing a

e) possible

fully-pled
ged I and

thou inti
mate–relat

ion.

Do creat *(6)*

a) ive artist

s reflect

the special
qualities

b) of their

countrie'

s landscap
ing as Tolstoi

immensely es

c) tablishing

War and Peace
epically mir

roring the
length and

d) depth of

Russia's

homestead
Whereas the

German-Jew

e) Heine felt e

qually at
home with

France's

f) more classi

cal trans
parent art

istic-land
scaping

s.

Just living

daily with a
beautiful wo

man brighten
s my poetic-

sensibility.

Neither (2)

a) more nor less

measuring

just the right
word-find's

a poetic-pro

b) cess intuit

ively self-
certaining

while also
space-impend

ing.

Voiced (4)

a) I couldn'

t feel it

as my voice
for it seem

b) ed to come

out of some

darkened place
housed in me

c) yet untouch

ably unanimous

ly there it rose
to an invis

ible height

d) beyond reach

even of my

landscap
ing eye-

length.

Pre-timing *(3)*

a) These cloud

s stretching-

out to the
full-length

b) of the sky'

s self-per

petuating
cotton-candy

softness
es as if pre-

c) timing him

self for a

most necess
ary bed-spac

ing sleep.

Many of *(2)*

a) Gaughin's

painting

s seem to
grow into them

selves as if
their landscap

b) ings had be

come called

to a new and
self-defin

ing identity-
cause.

Franz (3)

a) our almost 5-

year-old neigh

bor dressed
in such bright

b) self-distin

guishing color

s that even
his high-pitch

ed resound

c) ing voice

seemed as if
colored to

their self-
same intonat

ion.

In memory S. L. *(3)*

a) I'm convinced

he felt we'd

been intuned
to the same

b) wave-length

yet the re

ception on
our somewhat

out–used old–
fashioned

c) radio remain

ed often
statical

ly–disturb
ed.

Upside-down *(6)*

a) ness There

seems to be
a certain up

side-down

b) ness (remind

ing of Old
Father William)

about my most
essential-de

c) velopment

First a miss

ionary-Christ
ian followed

by a creation-

d) oriented poet

The stably-
escounced

wall-sitting
Humpty-Dum

e) ty expierien

ced that great

fall whereas
Old Father

William's
head-stand

f) ing hardly

changed his

toothless
ly-effective

life-style.

Windowed (3)

a) *A full land*

scaping from

the window
ed poet's

b) *room the nu*

merous house

s facing o
therwise dir

ections but
most especial

c) *ly those win*

dows witness

ing from their
time-seclud

ive look-out
post

s.

Will America (2)

a) learn once a

gain to honor

its poets Last
year's Nobel

Prize laureate

b) and that black

young lady
who stole Joe

Biden's inaug
ural on-dis

play.

Our grandson *(3)*

a) Aron burdened

from birth

with a learn–
deficiency

that left him

b) a year or two

behind his
learn–orient

ed contempor
aries But now

catching–up

c) with what his

contemporar
ies had

so thought
lessly left

behind.

Did they (2)

> *a) (those 2 to 5*
>
> year-olds)
>
> set the ex
> ample for the
>
> great Portu

> *b) gese and Span*
>
> ish discover
> ing their
>
> own at first
> self-limiting
>
> world-find
> ings.

Does it (3)

a) still remain

possible

(if listen
ing hard-e

b) nough) to

decipher the

echoing of the
oft unspoken-

c) thoughts of

a new famil

iarising-
friend

ship.

A translat (3)

a) *ed poem from*

whatever to

whatever lan
guage must

b) *quality-wise*

learn to

stand and sit
comfortab

ly on–its–
own–term

c) *s but not*

as the trans

later's own
poetising–

claim
s.

Perspective *(3)*

a) s Should my

unbeliev

able poetic-
prolific

b) ness be under

stood in a per

sonal auto
biographi

c) cal way and/or

as a new kind

of epic–kalei
doscopic–

poetry.

As a poetic (4)

a) ally inclined

historian

he always re
mained fascin

b) ated by those

medieval

wells especial
ly while e

choing their
century-old

c) concerns until

he learned

during those
14th century

plague-year
s Jews help re

d) sponsible for such

diseases were

cast-down to
their very depth

ed no-ways-
out.

Why did e *(3)*

a) rotically-

expressed-

love remain
such a minor

b) theme in Chin

ese poetry

whereas the
resplend

ant effects
of wine-drink

c) ing even drunk

enness often re

mained among
the most-essen

tial-worldly-
pleasure

s.

That small (3)

a) tiny-branched

tree right

in front-of
my window

b) ed light-

span now so

full of
blossoming

yellow bud
s that it

must have be

c) come satiat

ed with the
spring sun's

effusive-de
siring

s.

Those special (3)

a) colorings

Each word

must be siz
ed and weight

ed before it'

b) s allowed

to take its
pre-ordained

place But
sometime

c) s it's those

special color

ings that
make-all-the-

difference.

Curtain

s not only
establish a

certain de
gree of pri

vacy while
they also en

close a spec
ially unans

wered-inti
macy.

What remain *(7)*

a) s natural even

at its origin

ed-base and
what remain

b) s historical

ly-sourced

Women's espec
ially attend

ant to their
appearance-

c) sake and men'

s protective

"instinct
s" for love

and safety-

d) sake History

can most de
finitely

change a per
son and

e) even a nation'

s character

East German
's experience

with two dicta

f) torships has

created as
the Austrian

another
kind of Ger

man and Is

g) rael's exper

ience as a
Jewish state

has also created
another-kind

of Jew.

"It's just (4)

a) a cold spell"

she meant

the weather
would change

b) when its time

had come

Aren't our
moods some

how related

c) short-come

short-go
But even more

so when the

d) weather mood

s us in to
its own sover

eign-do
main.

Sometime *(3)*

    a) s tight poem

    s desire a

    release in
    to the flow

    b) of a rhyth

    mically other

    wise–source
    as when your

    hand's been

    c) grasped al

    most to its
    inexplicit

    breaking–
    point.

Distancing *(7)*

a) s Children

may fall as

leep while
counting the

b) heavenly

stars with

out realis
ing the space

they may need

c) to climb even

in search of
their still

most wondr
ous dream

d) s As a child

he used to

follow what
ever train

tracked from

e) Hartsdale

to Grand Cen
tral Station

until it
had become

f) completely

out-of-sight

That distanc
ing somehow

left him

g) with a vacant

feeling of
having been

self-abandon
ed.

A Prelude (3)

a) March 9 The

sky's bright

ening now e
ven before

b) I can answer

wordlessly–

inept The Good
Lord has fash

ioned His own
heavenly pan

c) oramic-design

s as we re

spond but ten
tatively

self-certain
ed.

It was some (4)

a) thing she kept

for herself

ashamed to
the very-depth

b) of a word

less–response

Pride often
leads to a

self–super
ior response

c) as those ri

der monument

s in the mid
st of a flour

ishing city
But with her

d) no available

response seem

ed adequate
even emotion

ally self–
sufficient.

Hearsay (4)

a) *'s often*

wrong–say

as our what
ever taste

b) *often differ*

s from anoth

er's response
Yet we most

often respond

c) *to such hear*

says with no
thing else to

rely upon
until actual

d) *ly confront*

ed with that

little known
person or

situation.

Does (3)

>*a) the im*
>
>mensity of
>Russia's 7–
>
>time-zone
>s and with

>*b) such a var*
>
>iety of peo
>
>ples at time
>s call for a
>
>strong and in
>tegrating

>*c) leader even*
>
>at expense
>
>of one's own
>most-cherish
>
>ed democrat
>ic-value
>
>s.

Personal (3)

a) ly experien

ced problem

atic–situat
ions only

b) deserve a

poetic–respon

se if their
timely–reach

c) extends e

ven beyond

one's own in
timate–re

sponse.

Responses (3)

a) Sometime

s an animal
response as

with Bileam'

b) s ass or that

rooster'

s 3-timed
biblical-in

c) itiative

s better acti

vating than
man's so-

called super
ior-respon

se.

Too highly (7)

a) position

ed or at the

other extreme
too low-down

b) poverty-strik

ened often

activates
an instinct

ual-behavior
that would

b) be better-

served with

in a more
self-protect

ive environ

d) ment "That

old grey mare

she ain't what
she used to

be" seems
most appro

e) priate when

every effort

seems not
only physical

ly ineffect

f) ive Is my

unusual poet
ic prolific

ness also a
kind of self–

g) compensat

ion for my e

qually-reali
sed daily-

felt physical-
deteriora

tion.

When the *(2)*

a) thought pro
cess and the

poetical
one running

on separate

b) *parallel*

tracks they'
ll seldom

reach a comm
on home-

base.

That cross- *(3)*

a) word-puzzle

kind of cur

ious learned-
intelligen

ce and I've

b) known at least

a handful of
such most all

excellent stud
ents as my

sister Doris

c) for example

yet also u
sually lack

ing what one
calls creativ

ity.

Can one call *(5)*

a) that a special

ly long and

intensive
love-relat

ion between
the nakedly

b) feminine

moon's effect

upon the ti
dal ocean

ed response

c) to her so

magnetical
ly releasing

encompass
ing know-

how Some es

d) pecial wo

men might
consider that a

lower-level
led animal–

like response

e) whereas it's

become an es
sential–part

of the creat
ive–process

itself.

Should one (5)

a) judge a creat

ive writer

on a one or
two-timed

b) especially

memorable

work as Matt
hew Arnold'

s Dover Beach

c) or Willa Cath

er's My Anton
ia and A Lost

Lady I would
prefer being

d) judged by my
entire poetic

work or is
such a pack

e) age-deal de
manding too-

much of a
critical-re

sponse.

Family photo (6)

a) graphs often

more reveal

ing than that
one-time appear

b) ance sake

would actual

ly justify
My father then

at the height

c) of his one-Trump-

like invest
ment–deal

s Doris look
ing to Lee

d) as a fully

loved and in

tellectual
ly acceptable–

partner Lois

e) the total op

posite to my
mother's pract

icality loving

f) ly embracing

and I gawky
and very much

adoles
cency.

Corona' (6)

a) s demanding

at least a

4-part re
sponse medi

cal social

b) and politi

cal oft deny

ing a unif
ied receptiv

ity And for

c) those young

sters play-
gaming as be

fore its low
ered its dead

d) ly age-effect

s For elder

Germans it re
sembles more

those war-end

e) bombings of

their citie'
s defense

less resist

f) ance No help

from vaccina
tions for

that kind of
allied-re

solve.

Big function (4)

a) s no longer

allowed at

Corona's re
quest should

b) be experien

ced not as a

grand self–
display but

as a means

c) of sharing

one's thank
fulness with

those inti
mately relat

d) ed and friend

s of a comm

only routed–
together

ness.

It sometime (3)

a) s seems help

ful (or may

be it shouldn'
t) being en

b) dowed with a

lesser-respon

sive-memory
when one be

comes critic
ised for a de

c) ficient-insen

sitive-behav

ior at the
very least

10 years
ago.

Dressed (3)

a) anew It snow

ed through

the night
dressed anew

b) in its purify

ing presence

that even Nath
aniel Pink

c) reconsider

ed his by

now somewhat
outused wint

er wardrobe.

I'm absolute (2)

a) ly certain

that no nat

ion ever be
came more

concerned
than Germany

b) about the

why when and
where of the

as yet unde
livered Corona

vaccine
s.

For Gary *(4)*

a) The Gypsies

a wandering
continually

persecuted

b) people divid

ed into over
a hundred

dialects with
out a unify

c) ing language

whose code of

behavior ap
pears to re

main primit
ive pre-10

d) commandment

s and also

without a
God-given land

to call its
own.

"It was snow (3)

    a) ing and it was

    going to snow"

    Wallace Steven
    s at his

    b) early (Harmon

    ium) poetic–

    best realis
    ing the self–

    perpetuat

    c) ing depth of

    his own
    shadowing

    identity–
    cause.

Operation (2)

a) *usually leave*

only scars be

hind as a
means of re

membering
the hurts

b) *and pains*

of one's

own accent
uating while

yet diminish
ing past.

Lost shad (6)

a) ows of a mani

fold past

Whatever be
came of him

b) my best his

tory student

at NYU so
taken (as he

wrote) by my

d) historical

lectures
that he chang

ed course
from a future

d) business car

eer He wrote

me (with most
certainly

his father

e) in the back

ground) while
I answered

that I'd
changed course

f) too from an

historical

relativist
ic one in

search of
higher-ideal

s.

Wettened- *(3)*

a) words once a

gain ground-

based from
a heavenly

b) release no

different

in-effect
from those

fallen autum
nal leav

c) ing behind

their stain

ed poetical
ly-flourish

ing side
walk

s.

Lazarus (2)

> *a) called-from-*
>
> the–dead
>
> as Jesus
> with a re
>
> turn–ticket
> must have

> *b) found his*
>
> once–aband
>
> oned world
> strangely–
>
> insuffic
> ient.

Self-dialog (4)

a) ued after Freud

If we're only

enabled to
understand

b) our once self

sufficient

past through
the eyes mind

and heart of
our tentative

c) ly otherwise-

present Does

that living–
past still re

tain the right
of viewing

d) our present-

day identity

with equally
so–called ob

jectivity.

Dated truths *(3)*

a) So-called

dated truth

s neverthe
less remain

sufficient

b) ly alive

as a subject
ive link bet

ween a many-
sided past

and our own

c) soon-to-be

dated time
and self-mir

oring pre
sent-day i

magining
s.

If certain (18)

> *a) peoples or*
>
> tribes have
>
> retained no
> recorded his
>
> tory of their

> *b) past Should*
>
> they themselv
> es be consider
>
> ed as non-exis
> tent as a day
>
> here in Otto

> *c) brunn departed*
>
> without a sin
> gle poem to
>
> verify its
> own situat

d) ed-identity

As Neil remem

bers more of
our at time

s common child

e) hood past

does only he and
not myself re

main histori
cally-relev

f) ant If as is

often main

tained at
funeral

s that he

g) or she will

continue to
be remember

ed through
their still

h) living friend

s and relat

ives When
they both die-

off is only

i) that stone

(if they
have one)

an assurance
that they

j) actually live

ed – is that

why Jewish
graves have

k) often been

so desecrat

ed especial
in the Nazi-

epoch When I

l) asked my Gypsy

colleague
Gary does his

people the
Sinti have

m) (as we Jews)

a particul

ar homeland
He answered

in a double-

n) sense Jaffin

esque sort-
of-way "We

Sinti have
been here in

o) Germany since

1417" I re

sponded "We
Jews were here

even before

p) the German

s and yet
they tried to

erase our
very indigen

q) ous-past

Jesus taught

us not to
look back to

our earthly

r) needs and ex

pectation
s but for

wards with
Him to our

resurrect
ing-future.

The more I *(5)*

  a) see and hear

  of my well-

  placed book
  s (and) poem

  b) s The more

  I should be

  come readied-
  to-die at

  death's most

  c) available

  time Though
  this daily

  love-life
  with Rosemar

d) ie and newly

dialogued

one with Poem
and my friend

s entices me

e) to a future

"More more
and more" of

a creative
time-spell.

The big move *(4)*

a) Preparing for

the big move

Our neighbor
s right–across–

b) the-way prepar

ing day by

day for their
big move com

ing in 2 month

c) s Rosemarie

and I know
all–too–well

that we've
also a big

c) move ahead

that can

only be help
ed by Christ'

s reassur
ing word

s.

Not only *(2)*

a) the aging

must learn to

live with
pain's a diff

icult bed-fell

b) ow always self-

sufficient
unable to real

ise the sleep
less needs

of other
s.

It's become (3)

    a) difficult

    to determine

    whether it'
    s raining

    b) snowing sleet

    ing or even

    hailing an o
    therwise cham

    c) eleoan-like

    approach to

    weather's
    changeabil

    ities.

I've become

as my father
so time-con

scious because
every minute'

s possibly
worth another

poem's recept
ivity.

Good-lang

uage's drown
ing under a

deluge of E
mails and the

like It's be
come the poet'

s job to re
establish its

former upstand
ing dignity.

This after

noon sun's
been cloud

ed-out of
its time-re

assuring
warmthed-in

tention
s.

Positivism *(3)*

a) Why are most

ladders dir

ectioned
(as far as

b) I can re

main certain

ed) upwards
while those

c) aimed downward

s seem as

if complete
ly overlook

ed.

Remember (5)

a) *ed What we*

remember

at age 83
of our past

b) *may appear*

for some as

more or less
completely

pleasing

c) *whereas for*

me it's those
dangerous

moments (and
we've all ex

d) perienced

those) that

nag at my
very-being

while perspect
ived by other

e) s may have

seemed noth

ing more or
less than a com

plete success-
story.

Belonging *(17)*

a) ness Today with

both husband
and wife oft

more than
half-employ

b) ed their o

ver-sensit

ive children
(as the former

kibbutz ones)

c) may feel a

sense of
where do I

really be
long These

d) days with so

many migrant

children dis
possessed

of both par

e) ents while

growthed in
a foreign

land with a
strange un

f) known lang

uage and o

therwise cus
toms may oft

g) be asking them

selves Who am

I and where
do I really

h) belong Or is

our instinct–

for–life Mo
ther–Courage–

like continu

i) ally overcom

ing such i
dentity-pro

blems Reowned
infants often

j) adopted out of

slum–street

condition
s (and I've

known several

k) of these) u

sually "forget"
their so–call

ed biological–
parents Those

l) Jewish

transport–
children

with parent
s killed in

m) The Holocaust

most often

grew–up in a
foreign non–

Jewish land

n) and household

and the most
famous one

who then be
came America'

o) s foreign minis

ter long foreign

ed as well to
her mothered

Jewish–identi
ty Does my

p) christen

ing reborn

text then re-
identify me

as a Christ
ian but then

o) my feeling

ness keeps re

minding me of
my continu

ing Jewish-her
itage.

While dia (2)

a) *loguing these*

early morning

poems the mid–
March darkness

has receded
leaving both

b) *Poem and myself*

with the en

lightened
words for

this quietly
oncoming-day.

While (4)

a) Columbus'

so-called

discovery-
of-America

b) has been

question

ed even on
historical

grounds and
as we now

c) realise the

saintly Chris

topherus
never really

existed must
we rewrite a

d) history that

has been writ

ing-us-through
now centurie

s-long.

Actually *(3)*

a) the most quest

ionable of

punctuat
ion marks re

b) mains the

closing final

ising–period
while truth

continues
on unknowing

c) just how far

its question

ings should
become time

ly–limited.

Has this pre- *(4)*

a) spring day be

come Corona-

masked as
well The tree

b)s still bare

ly leaf-touch

ed and des
pite the first

ground-based

c) flowering

s this land
seems hardly

life-recept
ive.

Are these (3)

a) *wintered bird*

s (the black

twig-bearing
ones) already

b) *nesting or*

have some of

the migrating
ones return

ed with the

c) *human migrant*

s rebirthing
a land long

since half-a
bandoned.

David Poem *(3)*

a) will continue

to chose you

because you'
re by far

b) the most ex

perienced

of craftmen
as that Carrara

c) marble chose

Michelangelo

to release it
from its pre–

angel marble
d–hold.

Poem and I *(2)*

> *a) both further*

> ed on this

> time-enclos
> ing mid–March

> morning's ex
> istencial feel

> *b) ing of being*

> direction

> ed for a book–
> ending finali

> sed express
> iveness.

I don't be (6)

a) lieve as that

veterinar

ian's Love of
Animals expos

b) ure of 3rd

children in

a human marr
iage as being

really occasion

c) ally ille

gitimate Neith
er husband nor

wife would have
been interest

d) ed in reveal

ing such a

concealed–
truth nor

would that

e) 3rd child as

Matthew and
myself Such

fake and false
"knowledge"

f) may neverthe

less improve

the sales of
such a "re

vealing" un
truth.

Change-of- *(5)*

a) pace The vague

across-the-

way window
ed-appear

b) ance of that

young tradit

ional family
with only 2

children

c) (no problem

here of a
3rd one)

helps me
think and

d) feel my way back

to our many

early move
s in what

e) would never

theless prove

to be a lov
ing and last

ing-marriage.

March 11, 2021
In Nomine
Domini!

P. S.

Transitional (2)

a) times as these

remain among

the most wind-
blown as well

Is that some
how symbolic

b) ally express

ive of their

often self-
deceptive

changeabili
ties.

Jesus continu *(5)*

a) ally required

absolute obed

ience of his
disciple

b) s well real

ising their

continual
off-pathed

ways even at

c) Golgatha

Does it re
main as wish

ful thinking
that I'm now

d) primarily

poetising

the beautie
s of His

Creation
daily living

e) out of His

loving-for

giveness Is
that really

enough?

At first

I hear only
what I want

ed to hear
Now I've be

come so gen
uinely half-

deaf that I'
m not even able

to hear that
anymore.

Have nation (5)

a) s really be

come depend

ent only on a relig
ion indigenous

b)ly theirs That'

s perhaps why

Chinese Confu
cianism (not

really a re

c) ligion) has

more deeply
formed their

raison d'être
than Indian

d) Buddhism

spiritually

Chinese-trans
formed Yet now

Christian

e) ity's beginn

ing to pene
trate their

most souled-
being.

Poetry books by David Jaffin

1. **Conformed to Stone,** Abelard-Schuman, New York 1968, London 1970.

2. **Emptied Spaces,** with an illustration by Jacques Lipschitz, Abelard-Schuman, London 1972.

3. **In the Glass of Winter,** Abelard-Schuman, London 1975, with an illustration by Mordechai Ardon.

4. **As One,** The Elizabeth Press, New Rochelle, N. Y. 1975.

5. **The Half of a Circle,** The Elizabeth Press, New Rochelle, N. Y. 1977.

6. **Space of,** The Elizabeth Press, New Rochelle, N. Y. 1978.

7. **Preceptions,** The Elizabeth Press, New Rochelle, N. Y. 1979.

8. **For the Finger's Want of Sound,** Shearsman Plymouth, England 1982.

9. **The Density for Color,** Shearsman Plymouth, England 1982.

10. **Selected Poems** with an illustration by Mordechai Ardon, English/Hebrew, Massada Publishers, Givatyim, Israel 1982.

20. **Sunstreams** with an illustration by Charles Seliger, Shearsman Books, Exeter, England 2007 and Johannis, Lahr, Germany.

21. **Thought Colors,** with an illustration by Charles Seliger, Shearsman Books, Exeter, England 2008 and Johannis, Lahr, Germany.

22. **Eye–Sensing,** Ahadada, Tokyo, Japan and Toronto, Canada 2008.

23. **Wind-phrasings,** with an illustration by Charles Seliger, Shearsman Books, Exeter, England 2009 and Johannis, Lahr, Germany.

24. **Time shadows,** with an illustration by Charles Seliger, Shearsman Books, Exeter, England 2009 and Johannis, Lahr, Germany.

25. **A World mapped-out,** with an illustration by Charles Seliger, Shearsman Books, Exeter, England 2010.

26. **Light Paths,** with an illustration by Charles Seliger, Shearsman Books, Exeter, England 2011 and Edition Wortschatz, Schwarzenfeld, Germany.

27. **Always Now,** with an illustration by Charles Seliger, Shearsman Books, Bristol, England 2012 and Edition Wortschatz, Schwarzenfeld, Germany.

28. **Labyrinthed,** with an illustration by Charles Seliger, Shearsman Books, Bristol, England 2012 and Edition Wortschatz, Schwarzenfeld, Germany.

29. **The Other Side of Self,** with an illustration by Charles Seliger, Shearsman Books, Bristol, England 2012 and Edition Wortschatz, Schwarzenfeld, Germany.

30. **Light Sources,** with an illustration by Charles Seliger, Shearsman Books, Bristol, England 2013 and Edition Wortschatz, Schwarzenfeld, Germany.

31. **Landing Rights,** with an illustration by Charles Seliger, Shearsman Books, Bristol, England 2014 and Edition Wortschatz, Schwarzenfeld, Germany.

32. **Listening to Silence,** with an illustration by Charles Seliger, Shearsman Books, Bristol, England 2014 and Edition Wortschatz, Schwarzenfeld, Germany.

33. **Taking Leave,** with an illustration by Mei Fêng, Shearsman Books, Bristol, England 2014 and Edition Wortschatz, Schwarzenfeld, Germany.

34. **Jewel Sensed,** with an illustration by Paul Klee, Shearsman Books, Bristol, England 2015 and Edition Wortschatz, Schwarzenfeld, Germany.

35. **Shadowing Images**, with an illustration by Pieter de Hooch, Shearsman Books, Bristol, England 2015 and Edition Wortschatz, Schwarzenfeld.

36. **Untouched Silences**, with an illustration by Paul Seehaus, Shearsman Books, Bristol, England 2016 and Edition Wortschatz, Schwarzenfeld.

37. **Soundlesss Impressions**, with an illustration by Qi Baishi, Shearsman Books, Bristol, England 2016 and Edition Wortschatz, Schwarzenfeld.

38. **Moon Flowers**, with a photograph by Hannelore Bäumler, Shearsman Books, Bristol, England 2017 and Edition Wortschatz, Schwarzenfeld.

39. **The Healing of a Broken World**, with a photograph by Hannelore Bäumler, Shearsman Books, Bristol, England 2018 and Edition Wortschatz, Cuxhaven.

40. **Opus 40**, with a photograph by Hannelore Bäumler, Shearsman Books, Bristol, England 2018 and Edition Wortschatz, Cuxhaven.

41. **Identity Cause**, with a photograph by Hannelore Bäumler, Shearsman Books, Bristol, England 2018 and Edition Wortschatz, Cuxhaven.

42. **Kaleidoscope**, with a photograph by Hannelore Bäumler, Shearsman Books, Bristol, England 2019 and Edition Wortschatz, Cuxhaven.

43. **Snow-touched Imaginings**, with a photograph by Hannelore Bäumler, Shearsman Books, Bristol, England 2019 and Edition Wortschatz, Cuxhaven.

44. **Two-timed**, with a photograph by Hannelore Bäumler, Shearsman Books, Bristol, England 2020 and Edition Wortschatz, Cuxhaven.

45. **Corona Poems**, with a photograph by Hannelore Bäumler, Shearsman Books, Bristol, England 2020 and Edition Wortschatz, Cuxhaven.

46. **Spring Shadowings**, with a photograph by Hannelore Bäumler, Shearsman Books, Bristol, England 2021 and Edition Wortschatz, Cuxhaven.

47. **October: Cyprus Poems**, with an illustration by Odilon Redon, Shearsman Books, Bristol, England 2021 and Edition Wortschatz, Cuxhaven.

48. **Snow Dreams**, with a photograph by Hannelore Bäumler, Shearsman Books, Bristol, England 2022 and Edition Wortschatz, Cuxhaven.

49. **Ukraine Poems**, with a painting by Alfons Röllinger, Shearsman Books, Bristol, England 2022 and Edition Wortschatz, Cuxhaven.

Book on David Jaffin's poetry: Warren Fulton, **Poemed on a beach,** Ahadada, Tokyo, Japan and Toronto, Canada 2010.